Ruth Bader Ginsburg Ruth Bader G
insburg Ruth Bader Ginsburg Ru
Ruth Bader Ginsburg Ruth Bader G
insburg Ruth Bader Ginsburg Ru
Ruth Bader Ginsburg Ruth Bader G
insburg Ruth Bader Ginsburg Ru
Ruth Bader Ginsburg Ruth Bader G
insburg Ruth Bader Ginsburg Ru
Ruth Bader Ginsburg Ruth Bader G

A SHORT BIOGRAPHY OF RUTH BADER GINSBURG

A SHORT BIOGRAPHY OF
Ruth Bader Ginsburg

Antonia Felix

 **BENNA** BOOKS

Carlisle, Massachusetts

A Short Biography of Ruth Bader Ginsburg

Series Editor: Susan DeLand
Written by: Antonia Felix

978-1-944038-69-4

FRONT COVER: *Ruth Bader Ginsburg*, 2010
Photograph
The Collection of the Supreme Court of the United States

BACK COVER: *Ruth Bader Ginsburg and husband, Marty,
with their daughter, Jane, in 1958*
Photograph
The Collection of the Supreme Court of the United States

Published by Benna Books
an imprint of Applewood Books, Inc.
Carlisle, Massachusetts 01741

To request a free copy of our current catalog
featuring our best-selling books, write to:
Applewood Books, Inc.
P.O. Box 27
Carlisle, Massachusetts 01741
Or visit us on the web at: www.awb.com

10 9 8 7 6 5 4 3 2 1
MANUFACTURED IN THE UNITED STATES OF AMERICA

"OYEZ! OYEZ! OYEZ!" CALLED OUT the marshal of the United States Supreme Court on October 4, 1993, using the court's traditional word (OH-yay) for "Hear Ye." On that notable day in American history, associate justice Ruth Bader Ginsburg took her seat on the bench to become the second woman to serve on the court since its first assembly in 1790. The first woman justice, Sandra Day O'Connor, had been serving for twelve years and would retire in 2006, leaving Ruth the only woman on the bench for three years until Sonia Sotomayor joined the court in 2010. In 2019, Ruth, Sonia, and Elena Kagan are the three women on the nine-person Supreme Court, and, a lifelong champion of equal gender rights, Ruth has envisioned that one day an all-woman court will be as normal as an all-male court once was. "We've had nine men for most of the country's history and no one thought that there was anything wrong with that," she said.

Before ascending to the Supreme Court, Ruth established herself as a trailblazer for gender rights by winning landmark anti-discrimination cases at that very court in the 1970s. Her work in those years earned her a comparison as the Thurgood Marshall of gender equality law, connecting her to the civil rights lawyer, who, before becoming a Supreme Court justice, had argued momentous civil rights cases before that court. Ruth's career evolved from law school professor and lawyer to federal judge when President Jimmy Carter appointed her to the U.S. Court of Appeals for the D.C. Circuit. After thirteen years on that bench, she was appointed by President Bill Clinton to the Supreme Court, where her opinions and eloquent yet stinging dissents have become legendary.

Ruth Bader Ginsburg was born Joan Ruth Bader in Brooklyn, New York, on March 15, 1933, to Nathan and Celia Amster Bader. The "Joan" was dropped when she entered a kindergarten class in which several other girls had the same name. Ruth's father, Nathan Bader, worked in the family business, Samuel Bader and Sons, a shop in Manhattan's garment district that made affordable furs for the working class. After the death of their father, Nathan and his brother Isadore partnered in the business and renamed it Nathan Bader, Inc.

Nathan left Odessa in Tsarist Russia in 1909, a thirteen-year-old fleeing the anti-Jewish uprisings to begin a new life in the United States. Ruth's grandfather came to the United States first to earn passage for the rest of the family. Later her grandmother arrived with Nathan and his three brothers. Their older sister was already married and she and her husband also emigrated. The Baders were among the two-million Jews who emigrated from Eastern Europe between 1900 and 1914. Celia was the first-born child in America to parents who had also left Eastern Europe, landing in Manhattan's Lower East Side to raise their already large, Yiddish-speaking family. Though Celia had excellent grades, her potential was thwarted by the family's decision to channel their resources into her older brother's prospects and education. Celia graduated high school at age fifteen and began working as a bookkeeper in the garment district to help earn money for her brother's education at Cornell University where he was enrolled in the forestry program.

The square-mile area of the Lower East Side in New York City was home to nearly 380,000 people in 1910, most of whom were Eastern European Jews like Ruth's ancestors.

Celia quit her job when she married Nathan, and the couple had their first child, Marilyn, in 1927. One year after Ruth came along, six-year-old Marilyn died from meningitis, leaving a pall of grief in the household. Marilyn was gone, but her nickname for Ruth, Kiki (named for her being a rambunctious, kicky baby), stayed on throughout Ruth's childhood and beyond. The lingering tragedy was softened by the togetherness of the large Bader-Amster extended family, a clan of aunts, uncles, and cousins who made up the heart of Ruth's Brooklyn world. The Baders had settled on East 9th Street in Flatbush, a working-class neighborhood of predominantly Jewish, Irish, and Italian immigrant families that offered green space and quiet as opposed to the crowded city grit of Manhattan's Lower East Side.

One of Ruth's most cherished memories of growing up is sitting on her mother's lap while Celia read to her. She also loved their trips to the library, where each week she selected a new stack of five books to take home. Life was full of exploring all the culture Brooklyn had to offer, including season tickets to children's performances at the Brooklyn Academy of Music and an early exposure to opera, both of which grounded Ruth's passion for music. She studied piano, played cello in high school, and dreamed of being one of the singers who graced stages like the Metropolitan Opera. "If I could have any talent God could give me, I would be a great diva," she later said. "But unfortunately I am a monotone and I only can sing in the shower and in my dreams."

Ruth's love for opera and the arts was seeded in Brooklyn, but her success in the law—and in life—began with her mother. Celia, whose proudest memories were of marching in New York's suffrage parades, instilled in Ruth the value of being independent. She shared her admiration for strong women like Eleanor Roosevelt, Hadassah founder Henrietta

Ruth's love of opera would culminate in a speaking part in *The Daughter of the Regiment* and supernumerary roles with the National Opera in Washington, D.C., in the 1990s and 2000s.

Szold, Zionist and writer Emma Lazarus, whose poem "The New Colossus" is etched on the Statue of Liberty, and social services pioneer Lillian Wald. Nurturing a daughter's independence was not the typical advice from mothers in the late 1940s and early 1950s, and it made all the difference for Ruth:

> *"This was an era when the expectation was [that] a girl should meet Prince Charming and marry and live happily ever after. My mother thought, well, that would be okay if Prince Charming came along, but I should be able to fend for myself."*

"What is the difference between a bookkeeper in the garment district and a Supreme Court justice? One generation, my mother's life and mine," Ruth said.

Celia's second life lesson impacting Ruth's future, especially her style as a litigator and judge, was to be a lady. By that she meant, Ruth explained, "Don't give way to emotions that sap your energy, like anger. Take a deep breath and speak calmly." Ruth's measured and steady demeanor, her habit of pausing momentarily before answering a question, is evident in court and during her public appearances.

As a student at James Madison High School, Ruth was a beautiful, blue-eyed, five-foot-three baton twirler in the pep squad, on the staff of the school newspaper, and member of the honor society. She won honors in her confirmation class at East Midwood Jewish Center and gave sermons at summer camp in upstate New York every year. But the times brought their share of darkness as well, such as American anti-Semitism on display. During a family drive in Pennsylvania, the family passed a resort carrying a sign that read "No dogs or Jews allowed." The worst times were the years at home as Ruth's mother struggled in her battle with cervical cancer. Diagnosed just as Ruth began her freshman year of high school,

Ruth did her homework at her mother's bedside throughout her mother's battle with cancer because she knew it pleased her to see her study.

Celia endured the multiple surgeries and worsening pain of the disease that would take her life. She died one day before Ruth's graduation at just forty-seven years old. Rather than attend her graduation ceremony and receive her academic medals, Ruth stayed home to mourn the loss of the mother who had armed her with the strength to persist, to be her own person, and to never give up.

In the fall of 1950, a few weeks after Celia's death, Nathan packed up Ruth's suitcases and drove her upstate to Ithaca, where Ruth enrolled at Cornell University on a full scholarship. She put her strong discipline to work to become one of the top students in her class.

Three mentors at Cornell stand out as major influences on her life and work, arguing famed novelist Vladmir Nabokov, whom she credits for transforming the way she reads and writes. As her literature professor, Nabokov showed Ruth how words could paint pictures and how "the right word in the right order . . . could make an enormous difference in conveying an image or an idea," she said.

Ruth was research assistant to another mentor, her constitutional law professor Robert E. Cushman, who raised her consciousness about the dangers of the Cold War–era Red Scare. While researching Senator Joseph McCarthy's efforts to root out Communists and alleged subversives in the government and film industry, Ruth uncovered the two lessons Cushman was eager for her to learn. First, the country was betraying its most fundamental values, and second, "legal skills could help make things better, could help to challenge what was going on," Ruth said. Her immersion into these events at the height of the Cold War may have awakened a sense of civil rights— and how the law can protect them—that would explain her choice to one day fight for gender rights.

Milton Konvitz taught a wildly popular

At Cornell, Ruth majored in government.

Milton Konvitz reinforced Ruth's new interest in civil liberties.

course called American Ideals. His lectures, she said, taught her about "our nation's enduring values and . . . how lawyers could remind lawmakers that our Constitution shields the right to think, speak, and write."

Ruth also led an active social life in college, going to movies and horseback riding, performing in a musical revue, and joining in activities in the Alpha Epsilon Phi sorority. Her most significant outing as a seventeen-year-old freshman, however, was a blind date on which she met a tall, handsome sophomore named Marty Ginsburg. They hit it off and began dating steadily, growing as friends through their mutual interests—which included opera. Marty was struck by Ruth's beauty *and* her intellect, which separated him from the pack for Ruth. She had not expected to meet a college man who was so confident in himself that he reveled in championing her to help her achieve her greatest potential. To Ruth, Marty

Marty Ginsburg was a varsity golfer at Cornell and shared his passion for the sport with his parents.

was "the first guy ever interested in me because of what was in my head," and when Marty proposed to her, she said yes. She considers it the best decision she ever made.

Ruth and Marty were married in the Ginsburgs' large home on Long Island shortly after Ruth graduated from Cornell in June 1954. Marty's parents were thrilled and became second parents to Ruth in a deeply supportive way, and the affection was mutual. Her new father-in-law, Morris Ginsburg, was an outgoing and vibrant man who had worked his way up from an eighth-grade education to become the vice president of a national department store chain. As undergraduates at Cornell, Ruth and Marty made a plan to enter the same field so that their lives would be connected in every way. Once they decided to become lawyers, Marty headed to Harvard Law and Ruth, one year behind him, applied and was also accepted. Harvard Law had only opened its doors to women four years earlier in 1950, and their numbers were slim. When Ruth enrolled in 1956, she was one of only nine women in a class of five hundred, an achievement that spoke to her outstanding academic record.

Ruth and Marty's grand plan about attending Harvard Law together took a detour when Marty was called to duty in the army reserves after finishing his first year of school. They spent the next two years on a virtual honeymoon at Fort Sill, Oklahoma, learning about each other without the distractions and pressures of school or family. They were an unusual couple, not as East Coast folks plunked down in Oklahoma, but as a pair who lived out the idea of equality day by day, both respecting and supporting each other's goals and careers. Ruth was working as a clerk at the time, but both she and Marty knew that she would begin law school when they returned and venture into whatever new life her law degree would lead her. They began their own family in those gap years, as Ruth called them, with the birth of Jane in the summer of 1955. When Marty's duties were finished the following year, they returned to Cambridge, Massachusetts.

In the fall of 1956, Ruth began her first year at Harvard Law and Marty entered his second year of the three-year program. Everything changed when Marty was diagnosed with testicular cancer and, very ill, could not attend class. In spite of the poor odds for his recovery, he and Ruth stayed optimistic. While Marty dealt with his heavy schedule of surgeries and radiation treatments, Ruth collected notes from his classmates, typed his senior paper as he dictated it to her from the couch—all while caring for their baby and attending her own classes. Much to their joy, Marty beat the odds and recovered. He cheated death, Ruth later said.

Both Marty and Ruth would face more medical crises during their long, prosperous marriage.

Marty's illness and the complications of life as a mother and law student did not slow down Ruth's ever-rising academic success. That first year she leaped over a competitive hurdle to make Law Review and finished among the top ten students in her class. Marty had been right all along to believe in her.

At the end of Ruth's second year at Harvard Law, she transferred to Columbia University Law School in order to move to New York with Marty. Fresh out of law school, he had taken a job at a major law firm, and Ruth supported the move completely. In the spring of 1959 she graduated from Columbia Law—in a class containing only twelve women—and tied for first in her class. That distinction should have won her a Supreme Court clerkship or job at a distinguished firm, but women were still the exception in the field. Ruth was trying to get into law with three strikes against her as a Jew, a woman, and a mother. "That combination was a bit too much," she said.

Ruth had an ally in her Columbia Law

In the 1950s, when women were hired at law firms, if at all, they were often offered jobs as secretaries or librarians rather than associates.

professor Gerald Gunther, who called dozens of judges to find her a clerkship on a federal court. After many rejections, he finally convinced Judge Edmund Palmieri of the U.S. District Court for the Southern District of New York to hire her. Following her successful clerkship, Ruth spent two years researching civil procedure in Sweden as part of a project at Columbia Law School. That work made an important impact, giving her a front-seat view of Sweden's feminist ideas about men and women taking equal responsibilities for raising children and earning incomes.

In 1963 she landed her first teaching job at Rutgers School of Law, where she would teach for nine years. In her second year she became pregnant, which seemed like a miracle after Marty's bout with cancer. Afraid of not being hired back if the administration learned she was pregnant, she wore baggy clothes to hide her figure. Once her new contract

Ruth found gender discrimination embedded in the law, such as a 1968 property law textbook that stated, "After all, land, like woman, was meant to be possessed."

was in hand, she announced the news to her colleagues, and her son James was born in September 1965. Ruth and Marty's family had grown, but three years later, Ruth's father died. He had lived to see his daughter become a happy wife and mother and achieve the rare feat of becoming a law professor at a time when very few women were in the field, but not long enough to see Ruth's history-making accomplishments as a litigator, judge, and Supreme Court justice.

In 1971, her last year teaching at Rutgers, Ruth became involved with the New Jersey chapter of the American Civil Liberties Union (ACLU). Marty, a prominent tax attorney and adjunct instructor at New York University Law School, had shown her a case in which a man was denied a small tax break for the homecare services he hired to take care of his aging mother while he was at work. Tax law did not allow single men who had never married to take the deduction. Ruth and Marty argued the gender discrimination case, *Moritz v. Commissioner of Internal Revenue*, on behalf of the ACLU in a federal appeals court and won. Ruth's work expanded the following year when she co-founded the ACLU's Women's Rights Project and again in 1973 when she became one of ACLU's four General Counsel.

In her decade at the ACLU, Ruth participated in more than three hundred gender discrimination cases—arguing six before the Supreme Court. She won five of those landmark decisions, beginning with *Frontiero v. Richardson* (1973). The historic case that marked the turning point in American law took place in 1971, just when Ruth was getting started at the ACLU. Her brief for *Reed v. Reed* convinced the Supreme Court that an Idaho law about administering an estate after a relative's death was unconstitutional because it discriminated based on gender. In this case, grieving mother Sally Reed was denied the right to administer the estate of her son, who had died without leaving a will. State law dictated that, in appointing administrators, males must be preferred to females. Ruth's brief, based on and expanding the ideas in her Moritz brief, argued that this discrimination violated the Equal Protection Clause of the Fourteenth Amendment. Equal protection for women and men, she asserted, means males cannot be preferred to females. The justices unanimously agreed and struck down the Idaho law.

With her *Reed v. Reed* brief, Ruth changed the course of history. The landmark decision marked the first time that the Supreme Court declared a sex-based law unconstitutional under the Equal Protection Clause.

Ruth used the same argument in the first case she argued before the Supreme Court. In *Frontiero v. Richardson*, Air Force Lieutenant Sharron Frontiero was suing the U.S. Secretary of Defense over

"I did see myself as kind of a kindergarten teacher in those days because the judges didn't think sex discrimination existed," Ruth said of her 1970s court cases.

the denial of benefits for her husband. The government had refused her request, stating that she would have to prove that her husband was a dependent, even though servicemen did not have to prove the same about their wives. Ruth argued that this gender discrimination violated the Equal Protection Clause. Just as in her *Reed v. Reed* brief, she applied the same reasoning that Thurgood Marshall had used to argue that racial discrimination violated the Equal Protection Clause in *Brown v. Board of Education*. Addressing the justices, Ruth made the point crystal clear: "Why did the framers of the 14th Amendment regard racial [discrimination] as odious? Because a person's skin color bears no necessary relationship to ability. Similarly, . . . a person's sex bears no necessary relationship to ability." The justices agreed, 8 to 1.

In the Court's *Frontiero v. Richardson* opinion, Justice William Brennan famously declared that the traditional legal treatment

Ruth and her ACLU colleagues sought to educate judges and lawmakers that the status quo of gender discrimination disadvantaged their daughters and grand-daughters.

of gender, based on an attitude of "romantic paternalism," often "put women not on a pedestal, but in a cage."

In *Weinberger v. Wiesenfeld*, a 1975 Supreme Court case that Ruth described as dear to her heart, a widower was denied Social Security benefits to take care of his infant after his wife died in childbirth. At the time, the benefit was given only to women who had lost their husbands, not men who had lost their wives. The court unanimously ruled that this discrimination was unconstitutional. Getting rid of discriminatory laws meant first changing the underlying attitudes that created them. Ruth realized that the women's rights movement of the 1970s that made the shifts in the national consciousness had to occur before judges and lawmakers would be prepared to act. She admitted that the groundbreaking work on gender law may not have been possible without the social changes of the decade:

This case and many others showed that gender discrimination harmed men as well as women by forcing them into distinct gender roles.

"What caused the Court's understanding to dawn and grow? Judges do read the newspapers and are affected, not by the weather of the day . . . but by the climate of the era."

The times and Ruth's activities in them made an impression on her daughter, Jane, as evidenced in the remarks Jane made in her high school yearbook in her graduation year of 1973. True to her generation, Jane's expectations and aspirations about women's roles in society had expanded far beyond those of her mother's 1950s generation. Under the heading "Ambition," Jane's yearbook stated—prophetically—that she wanted "to see her mother appointed to the Supreme Court." And if that wasn't ambitious enough, the next statement read, "If necessary, Jane will appoint her." Jane wasn't the president of the United States when her mother was nominated to the Supreme Court, but she did build a distinguished career in both her parents' footsteps. She attended Harvard Law School, where she made Law Review, like Ruth, and became a professor at the Columbia University School of Law. Jane married attorney George Spera in 1981, and they have two children and one grandchild. Ruth and Marty's son, James, followed the family's musical interests to launch Cedille Records, a classical music label, and he also has two children. James is married to composer and operatic soprano Patrice Michaels.

In 1972, Ruth left Rutgers to take a position at her alma mater, the Columbia University School of Law. She made her mark in legal history that year by becoming the first woman granted tenure at the school. Working through the decade at the vanguard of gender discrimination law, she gained national prominence and was appointed by President Jimmy Carter to become a judge on the U.S. Court of Appeals for the D.C. Circuit. Marty quit his job as a tenured professor at Columbia

In 1974, while teaching at Columbia Law School, Ruth coauthored *Sex-Based Discrimination*, the first law school casebook on the topic.

Law to move to Washington for Ruth's new position. In Washington, their lifestyle included regular visits to the National Opera and dinner parties featuring Marty's near-celebrity chef skills. Since early in their marriage, Ruth and Marty agreed that he should do the cooking. (Ruth wasn't much of a cook, as her family openly reminded her.) After Marty's death, as a tribute to him and his cooking talent, the wives of Ruth's colleagues put together some of Marty's recipes and published the cookbook titled *Chef Supreme*.

Ruth was forty-seven years old when she joined the D.C. Circuit, and over the next thirteen years she earned respect as a moderate judge and gained a lasting friendship with fellow judge Antonin Scalia. When her prominence put her on President Bill Clinton's short list for a nominee to the Supreme Court, Marty pulled out all the stops to enlist the support of everyone on his list of power brokers in law and academia. He had done the

Although often on opposing sides of a legal issue, Ruth and Antonin Scalia enjoyed a close friendship and shared a love for opera.

same years earlier to gather support for her nomination to the D.C. Circuit, and his efforts paid off both times. President Clinton chose Ruth, and she won over the Senate with a 96-to-3 confirmation vote. On August 10, 1993, at age sixty, Ruth was sworn in as the second woman and 107th member of the Supreme Court.

Ruth's reputation as a moderate-liberal justice has followed her through twenty-six years on the bench. Her opinions and dissents reflect her strong support of gender equality, the separation of church and state, and workers' rights. She wrote the majority opinion, for example, for the Court's groundbreaking 1996 decision on *United States v. Virginia*, another case centered upon the Equal Protection Clause, which opened the doors for women to enroll in the Virginia Military Institute.

An example of Ruth's singular voice of dissent came in 2000 when the court's majority decision favored George W. Bush over Al Gore in the presidential election

In 1999 Ruth won the Thurgood Marshall Award for her contributions to gender equality and civil rights.

decision. The final line of her dissent, which traditionally includes the word "respectfully," simply stated, "I dissent." In recent years her voice in favor of issues considered on the liberal spectrum of American politics have given her pop-star status, thanks to a young, engaged generation and the power of digital media.

While Supreme Court justices have typically been private figures in the background of American culture, Ruth has become a veritable celebrity with T-shirts, coffee mugs, Internet memes, and tattoos emblazoned with her image and taglines such as "Notorious R.B.G.," aligning her with the rapper Notorious B.I.G. The various jabots, or collars, she wears with her black robe, including one reserved only for dissenting opinions, have been replicated by accessory designers. Kate McKinnon portrays her regularly on *Saturday Night Live*, and in 2018 two films arrived in theaters—the documentary *RBG* and feature film *On the Basis of Sex*—in commemoration of Ruth's twenty-five years on the court.

Throughout her life, Ruth has met challenges with grace and strength, particularly the blow of Marty's death from cancer in 2010, which left her without her beloved best friend and partner of fifty-six years. In the preface to her 2016 book, *My Own Words*, Ruth wrote, "I do not have words adequate to describe my super smart, exuberant, ever-loving spouse." Their life together was a living example of equality as the normal state of things, as Marty remarked when Ruth was nominated to the Supreme Court: "I have been supportive of my wife since the beginning of time, and she has been supportive of me. It's not sacrifice; it's family."

In 2019, at eighty-six, Ruth has vowed to stay on the bench as long as she can do the job "full steam," and nothing has stopped her yet. A three-time cancer survivor, she works out with a trainer every week, is

Toward the end of his life, Marty had told a friend, "I think that the most important thing I have done is to enable Ruth to do what she has done."

the adoring grandmother of four, and is fulfilled in her Constitutional mission as a justice. She has remarked that regardless of the differences in opinion, ideology, or philosophy among her colleagues, they genuinely respect each other and enjoy each other's company . . . a wise model for us all.